Published by Creative Education
and Creative Paperbacks
P.O. Box 227, Mankato, Minnesota 56002
Creative Education and Creative Paperbacks
are imprints of The Creative Company
www.thecreativecompany.us

Design by The Design Lab
Production by Joe Kahnke
Art direction by Rita Marshall
Printed in the United States of America

Photographs by Alamy (A M Seward), Corbis (Vincent
Grafhorst/Minden Pictures), Dreamstime (Anekoho,
Chat9780, Dlrz4114, Svetlana Foote, Fotokev,
Andre Klaassen), iStockphoto (GlobalP, pjmalsbury),
Shutterstock (Aaron Amat, EcoPrint, Michael Maes,
Zorro12)

Library of Congress Cataloging-in-Publication Data
Bodden, Valerie.
Meerkats / Valerie Bodden.
p. cm. — (Amazing animals)
Summary: A basic exploration of the appearance, be-
havior, and habitat of meerkats, the African mammals
that live in mobs. Also included is a story from folklore
explaining why meerkats are always on the lookout.
Includes bibliographical references and index.
ISBN 978-1-60818-756-0 (hardcover)
ISBN 978-1-62832-364-1 (pbk)
ISBN 978-1-56660-798-8 (eBook)
1. Meerkat—Juvenile literature.
QL737.C235 B63 2017
599.74/2—dc23   2016004789

CCSS: RI.1.1, 2, 4, 5, 6, 7; RI.2.2, 5, 6, 7, 10;
RI.3.1, 5, 7, 8; RF.1.1, 3, 4; RF.2.3, 4

HC 9 8 7 6 5 4 3
First Edition PBK 9 8 7 6 5 4 3 2 1

MEERKATS

BY VALERIE BODDEN

CREATIVE EDUCATION • CREATIVE PAPERBACKS

Meerkats belong to the same animal family as mongooses

Meerkats are small

mammals. They stand on their back legs to watch for danger. If an eagle or hawk flies over, the meerkats dive into their **burrows**.

burrows holes or tunnels dug in the ground for use as a home

mammals animals that have hair or fur and feed their babies with milk

*Dark eye circles reflect, or
throw back, the bright sunlight*

Meerkats have long, thin bodies. They have brownish-gray fur with black patches around their eyes. Long, sharp claws on their toes help them dig burrows and catch **prey.**

prey animals that are killed and eaten by other animals

Most meerkats are about as long as a ruler. Their tails are almost as long as their bodies. They weigh less than a small house cat.

The stripes on a meerkat's back are different on each animal

Meerkats live in hot, dry areas of Africa. It can get up to 160 °F (71.1 °C) there during the day. At night, the temperature can drop to 40 °F (4.4 °C). Meerkats' burrows stay cool in the daytime. Their burrows are warm at night.

Meerkats have ears that can pinch shut to keep out sand

A good sense of smell helps a meerkat find food anywhere

Meerkats dig up **insects** to eat. Their favorites are grasshoppers, beetles, and **larvae**. Meerkats eat lizards and **rodents**, too. They even munch on dangerous scorpions!

insects small animals with three body parts and six legs

larvae the form some animals take when they hatch from eggs, before changing into their adult form

rodents small mammals with big teeth, such as mice and rats

*Young meerkats do not
go far from the burrow*

A meerkat mother gives birth to four to six **pups**. The pups cannot see or hear when they are born. They stay in the burrow and drink their mother's milk. After almost four weeks, the pups go outside. Meerkats can live about 10 years in the wild.

pups baby meerkats

A male and female called the alpha pair lead the mob

Meerkats live in family groups called mobs. Up to 40 meerkats live in a mob. Each mob guards its own **territory**. If two mobs meet, the meerkats will fight.

territory a space that is the home of one animal or one group of animals

Meerkats spend most of the day looking for food. One meerkat serves as the lookout. The lookout watches for danger. It barks or chirps to the others. Meerkats spend time cleaning each other's fur and playing, too.

Meerkats look for insects in trees and other nest sites

Some people travel to Africa to see meerkats in the wild. Others see them on TV or at zoos. It can be fun to watch these furry little mammals scurry around!

Meerkats love being in a group instead of by themselves

A Meerkat Story

Why are meerkats always on the lookout? People in Africa told a story about this. They said that Meerkat never watched where she was going. The other animals told her to be more careful. They warned her not to wake the Sleeping Stones. But one day, she crashed into the Stones. The Stones told her that, from then on, she would have to be the lookout for all animals.

Read More

Bateman, Helen, and Jayne Denshire. *Dangerous Creatures of the Deserts*. North Mankato, Minn.: Smart Apple Media, 2005.

Schuetz, Kari. *Meerkats*. Minneapolis: Bellwether Media, 2012.

Websites

Enchanted Learning: Meerkats
http://www.enchantedlearning.com/subjects/mammals/mongoose/Meerkatcoloring.shtml
This site has meerkat facts and a picture to print out and color.

San Diego Zoo Kids: Meerkat
http://kids.sandiegozoo.org/animals/mammals/meerkat
Learn more about meerkat pups and adults.

Note: Every effort has been made to ensure that the websites listed above are suitable for children, that they have educational value, and that they contain no inappropriate material. However, because of the nature of the Internet, it is impossible to guarantee that these sites will remain active indefinitely or that their contents will not be altered.

Index